The Millionaire
AUTHOR

"If you already have a book written—or you have one in you and just need to get it on paper—then you need to read this! I have watched first-hand how Peggy can take an author and build a million dollar business around their book. This will give you the inside secrets to make that happen for yourself!"
Brian Proctor, Proctor Gallagher Institute

"If you have a desire to be successful as an author read every word of Peggy McColl's book and put it into action now. She knows what she's talking about."
David Riklan, Founder—SelfGrowth.com

"If you are looking for the first, and possibly only, book to read if you want to figure out how to finance the rest of your life by writing, read this. This book has good solid advice and is laid out in a simple and easy to comprehend format. Peggy gives the outline of a very stable wealth-building strategy. The writing is clear and concise, and the concepts are easy to understand and implement. I would definitely recommend buying an extra copy & passing it along to someone you think would also appreciate being rich."
Judy O'Beirn, Creator & Best Selling Co-Author, *Unwavering Strength*

"Insightful, intuitive, a terrific motivator and THE expert in her field, Peggy's new book lays the pathway to success—for everyone—showing how to take your deepest passion, share it with the world, make a difference AND make money. Can it get any better than that? Yes, it can! You'll learn how to align yourself with the mindset of a bestselling author, build a brand and a business to free you to shine your light in the world, just as Peggy is doing right now. Oh, and did I mention, Peggy's a great Grandma, too?"

Janet Swift

"It's not enough just to become an author anymore . . . Don't be like the thousands so called "authors" that have piles of their books in the garage and can't figure out how to sell them. There is a specific formula to make your book into a business, and an even more exact formula to make your book make you a millionaire.

In <u>The Millionaire Author</u> Peggy McColl goes through many case studies and methods telling you exactly how todays new authors makes millions. If being "Just" an author isn't good enough for you.. Then the obvious choice is . . . <u>The Millionaire Author</u>."

Stephan Stavrakis, Positioning Strategist**,** Author, *The Only: How your company can become the obvious choice*

"There's only one way to turn a book into a multi-million dollar business. And that's to learn from someone who has done it over and over again. Peggy is the real deal. This book is the real deal. Read it, absorb it and ignite your million dollar future."

Steve Lowell, International Speaker & Professional Speaking Mentor

"Peggy has packed this book with exact, finite evidence that no matter what you presently think, there's nothing standing in your way of becoming a millionaire author. You will learn so much while feeling loved and worthy of success. Benefit from Peggy's many stories that will cause you to leap into massive action and create yourself as a millionaire author. With this book, the power is truly in your hands."

Trace Haskins, Marketing Dude & Coach

"Peggy McColl not only has what it takes to create great success by generating millions in personal income, but goes way beyond to another level by sharing and teaching what she knows with others to help them reach for their millions. If you are ready to receive what she is offering you—your life will be changed for the better forever! Go to , like I did, and take action on your future!"
    Bruce McGregor, The GPS Guy! Author and Success Coach

"<u>The Millionaire Author</u> is another fantastic book by Peggy McColl. Not just a great read but a book packed full of real and practical tools that truly help you to become the successful author you want to be. I personally love the Vibrational Alignment cards and their ability to consciously move you closer to your goal of becoming a New York Times Best Selling Author. I'm fine tuning my vibration because of them. Thank you Peggy, you've created another offering that will change lives."
    Kerrie Wearing—Author, *Soul Coach* and *Medium*

"Want the genuine, honest goods? Meet Peggy McColl. She always gives the best of what she knows--and she knows a lot! You couldn't do better than to read anything Peggy writes, and to work with her if you get the chance. She is amazing."
    Kathryn Jefferies, PhD, Author, *AWAKE: Education for Enlightenment*

"Peggy McColl gets that authorship and business go hand and hand. She is the master at teaching you how to turn your book into money making ideas that can create massive wealth in your life."
    Lisa Larter, Social Media Expert

"This book is your ticket to greater wealth and expansion. <u>The Millionaire Author</u> is filled with so much valuable wisdom and content that supports the reader way beyond just the words written in the book. You're going to get so many practical tips to help you magnify your wealth, and I'm truly blown away at Peggy's generosity in giving so much value away in this book. I especially love the chapter on expanding your wealth while you sleep! If you are someone who is into expanding your brand and business, I absolutely recommend this amazing book!"

Emmanuel Dagher

"Great book for beginners or professionals who want to learn how to make money writing. The book has an easy and conversational tone. The writing is clear and concise, and the concepts are easy to understand and implement. There are many nuggets of wisdom packed in this book. Peggy's writing style is engaging, quirky, upbeat and above all interesting . . . a book for anyone. I would highly recommend it."

Sharon Campbell-Rayment, International Best Selling Author, Speaker—The Horse & Soul Connection

"<u>The Millionaire Author</u> is packed full of secrets and strategies that you won't find anywhere else. If you would like to become a millionaire author, you owe it to yourself to read this book and put it's incredibly effective strategies into practice. Your author career will thank you."

Jennifer Colford, International Best Selling Author

"Peggy McColl has written a guidebook for authors that explores all avenues of publishing, marketing, and developing business strategies that expand your book into a huge revenue generator. The author shares her own experiences in a concise, easy to follow format that will save the reader many hours of study and many thousands of dollars as well. The simple, creative steps outlined in this book are pure genius and will put anyone in the driver's seat, whether first time author, or successful author who wants to expand their business to the next level. I highly recommend this book as a starting point for getting yourself on The Millionaire Author track!"

Kathi Casey, ERYT, CPI, The Healthy Boomer Body Expert, Amazon International Bestselling Author

"This book is filled with simple steps to become a published author and improve your life at the same time."

Annette Slater

"The Millionaire Author is THE place you need to go for a step-by-proven-step guide to making your book become a Best Seller and you a millionaire author. Peggy's advice and decades of wisdom gently lead you to success. A must have on any author's bookshelf as your own personal roadmap."

Banafsheh Akhlaghi, Esq. Internationally Acclaim Lawyer, Speaker, Professor and Social Entrepreneur

"I always have just two words of advice when anyone tells me about their book idea. Those two words? "Peggy McColl." Peggy understands how to turn an idea into a manuscript—and then how to turn that manuscript into a success. She knows a book market that is constantly evolving thanks to new technologies and new approaches to marketing. More than that, Peggy cares about people and The Millionaire Author is proof. Page after page of effective, up to the minute advice that anyone can put to work right now. Peggy has put it all there for any of us to run with."

Chris McKillop, Communications Consultant

"The Millionaire Author by Peggy McColl is a book that every author should have in his or her bookshelf. This is a brilliant book that covers wise and important information that you do *not want to miss out on especially if you want to become a successful author! I highly recommend you read this book."*

Julie Ringnes, Author and Founder of Lykke by Julie

"If you have dreamed of not only becoming a best-selling author, but also a financially abundant entrepreneur as a result, this book is a must read. The Millionaire Author *is your roadmap to success. To be the best, learn from the best and Peggy's achievements say it all."*

Faith Poe, International bestselling co-author, *Unwavering Strength*

"Peggy McColl is an absolute master at helping authors build successful businesses and her new book The Millionaire Author *will help you do just that! Peggy's genius is helping people believe in themselves, position themselves to attract amazing opportunities, and bring their messages into the world in a powerful way. Peggy has been instrumental in helping me personally become a successful author and I trust that her wisdom will help you too."*

Dina Proctor, Bestselling Author, *Madly Chasing Peace; How I went from Hell to Happy in Nine Minutes a Day*

"Wow, Peggy McColl has hit a home run with this wonderful book. If you have ever had the desire to write but wasn't sure how to get started, this book is your answer. Peggy provides simple steps to help you reach your dreams and the encouragement and care to let you know she is supporting you every step of the way. A must read!"

Alena Chapman, *Author, You Can't Escape From a Prison If You Don't Know Your In One: What is Blocking Your Freedom?"*

*"*The Millionaire Author *is full of actionable tips and advice that teach you how to become a best-selling author AND build a*

business around your book so you can make you money while you sleep. But it goes far beyond that.

Peggy has the unique ability to connect with her audience by sharing her personal experiences, along with real world examples, that help us break down the barriers that are holding us back from revealing the best-seller that lies within us.

Perhaps my favourite quote from the book is found right off the bat in chapter 1, and with the tools and information that Peggy shares with us in <u>The Millionaire Author,</u> I believe it! Peggy writes, "do you see the pattern here? There is no pattern! Any author can become a millionaire author." If you feel like you have a message to share with the world, don't hesitate. Pick up Peggy's latest book now! You won't regret it."

Roger Deveau, *Creator, The Launch Formula—The 10 steps to getting results and momentum in your business*

"Peggy McColl has done it again! I have read several of her books, and this is her best yet. If you want to learn how to write a book quickly, become a bestselling author, and create a profitable empire out of your book, <u>The Millionaire Author</u> is for you. And who better to learn from than someone who has done it all herself! Peggy's advice will change your life . . . I know it has changed mine."

Karen Strang Allen, Life Transformation Expert and Author, *Free to be me: Create a life you love from the inside out!*

"I was first introduced to Peggy McColl and her work very recently and was absolutely blown away. She has such a wealth of knowledge and really proves that anyone can achieve success. In her latest book, she provides wonderful background stories and insight on how to take the next step in launching your million dollar business. The best success comes in the form of giving great value to others. I would highly recommend reading this book! I absolutely cannot wait to apply what she teaches in my businesses! Thank you for such a phenomenal book, Peggy!"

Bradley Shavis, Entrepreneur and Life Coach

"Through her powerful, easy to understand teachings, Peggy has helped me create a book and a business that work together, that I am passionate about. I would not have the confidence or the belief that I could do what I am doing without her proof that it can be done and her strategies on how to do it—and have fun doing it! Thank you Peggy and <u>The Millionaire Author</u> for showing me the way!"

Ricci Reardin, Owner, The Puppy Academy

"This little book is packed full of simple yet powerful tips for understanding the mindset of a <u>Millionaire Author</u>. Peggy's unique ability to clearly articulate and illustrate just how her own personal magic works is at play here. She makes seemingly complex subjects fun and approachable. Read this book, and then read it again. Each read will reveal yet another nugget hidden inside."

Nancy Thiel Voogd, Founder of SpiralVision

"Peggy McColl hits another home run with her new book, <u>The Millionaire Author</u>. Peggy's books are always packed with useful information guaranteed to inspire you on your own Millionaire Author journey."

Jayne Blumenthal, JayneBlumenthal.com

"If you want to achieve great success as an author, study Peggy McColl's book now. To paraphrase a great quote: 'When you do today what other's won't, you will have tomorrow what other's don't.' Study this book and do what Peggy suggests."

Patrick Snow, International Best-Selling Author, Professional Keynote Speaker

The Millionaire AUTHOR

THE HIDDEN STRATEGIES TO TURN YOUR BOOK INTO A MILLION DOLLAR BUSINESS

Peggy McColl

Published by
Hasmark Publishing
1-888-402-0027 ext 101

© 2014 Peggy McColl All rights reserved

Disclaimer
Although the author and publisher have made every effort to ensure that the information in this book was correct at press time, the author and publisher do not assume and hereby disclaim any liability to any party for any loss, damage, or disruption caused by errors or omissions, whether such errors or omissions result from negligence, accident, or any other cause. This book is not intended as a substitute for the medical advice of physicians or any other professional. The reader should regularly consult the proper professionals in matters relating to his/her health, financial matters and particularly with respect to any symptoms that may require diagnosis or medical attention. The information in this book is not meant to supplement, not replace, proper investment training. The authors and publisher advise readers to take full responsibility for their safety, success and know their limits.

Copyedit by Philip S Marks

www.DocUmeantPublishing.com

Cover by Killer Covers

http://killercovers.com

Layout by DocUmeant Designs

www.DocUmeantDesigns.com

ISBN-13:978-1502881076
ISBN-10:1502881071

Dedication

To my grandson James who brings pure love, complete joy and an abundance of sunshine into my life.

Contents

Dedication iii

Foreword vii

Acknowledgements ix

Introduction xiii

Part I: The Millionaire Mindset - - - - - - - - - - - - - 5

Chapter 1. The Modern Day Gold Rush 7

Chapter 2. Get Out of Your Own Way 15

Chapter 3. Dream with Your Eyes and Ears Open . 23

Part II: Writing and Marketing - - - - - - - - - - - - 31

Chapter 4. So You Think You Can't Write 33

Chapter 5. Dare to Bake Cookies 41

Chapter 6. Reach Out and Touch Everyone 49

Part III: Cash is King — 57

Chapter 7. Unlimited Possibilities 59

Chapter 8. Earn Money in Your Sleep 65

Chapter 9. Open the Gates 71

Conclusion 77

About the Author 81

Foreword

YOU MADE AN EXCELLENT INVESTMENT by reading Peggy McColl's little book. *The Millionaire Author* is rich with valuable strategies to show you the steps you must take if you really want to live the life you desire. I've mentored Peggy for almost 30 years and she has done what she teaches in this book many times. I've watched Peggy grow from an unhappy, self-loathing office girl to a confident and powerful speaker who captures entire audiences. Peggy is the author of many books that climbed to the top of the world's book charts while she created a multi-million dollar business. This woman knows what she's talking about.

The information in this book is enormously valuable . . . study it and apply it . . . winning will be your reward. The success I have enjoyed over the past fifty years is due to following the advice of individuals who had already done what I wanted to accomplish. It is unfortunate but true that the vast majority of our population is blind to this obvious rule for success. Peggy not only has a unique way of teaching valuable life lessons that's she learned, these lessons that will give you everything you are looking for. Strange and marvelous things will begin to happen in your life with constant regularity by following

Peggy McColl's direction.

Don't let Peggy's rhetoric and warm conversational tone fool you, this book is so full of tips and tricks that you can start to capitalize on right now! Read this book through and make the decision to move forward. Then study the lessons Peggy teaches. Your return will be in exact proportion to your effort. You can become a millionaire author just like thousands of others. Study this book and invest in yourself by working with the author. You deserve the millionaire life of your dreams. What are you waiting for? Make the decision to make it happen and start moving forward. I will see you at the top of the best seller lists.

Bob Proctor

Acknowledgements

AS YOU WILL DISCOVER in this book my most important value is my family. My husband Denis, my son Michel and my grandson James are the inspiration behind everything I do and true blessings in my life.

I feel blessed to be sharing my life with my husband Denis, who I have a soul-connection with. What I love most about Denis is who he is . . . kind, loving, giving, generous, supportive, intelligent and respectful.

My son Michel is my biggest inspiration. Every now and then I attempt to tell Michel just how much I love him and how much he means to me, but seldom find the words to express the total, complete and unconditional love that I feel for him. (If you are a parent and you are reading this, you probably understand what I am trying to say.)

My grandson James, whom this book is dedicated to, lights up my world in ONLY beautiful and loving ways. His presence brings joy into the room. He makes me smile and laugh. He truly inspires me.

My blessings and family expands in more glorious ways . . . I have the wonderful love and support of my sister Judy O'Beirn, my nieces Amy Lusk and Jennifer Lusk-Gibson, my daughter-in-law Kayla Leon, my step-daughter Karine, my step-son-in-law Rob and my beautiful step-grandchildren Noah and Lila.

I feel overwhelmingly grateful for Bob Proctor, who wrote the Foreword for this book. I cherish his friendship and he has been my mentor for decades. Bob has taught me more about success than anyone. Period.

A special thanks to Jennifer Colford (also know as "Fabulous Jen") who jumped in whole-heartedly and helped create this book at lightening speed. She's amazing. She's gifted. And, I am grateful to her.

A big expression of gratitude to the Hasmark Publishing team run by my sister Judy O'Beirn along with my devoted niece Jennifer Gibson. Tapping into their brilliance and phenomenal service, both Judy and Jenn jumped in to help get this book into print edition quickly. I appreciate all you do.

Gratitude goes out to my mastermind buddy Arielle Ford, who shares weekly accomplishments and support. She inspires me to do more, give more and experience more.

My special friend Brian Proctor, who, like his Dad, always gives. He is the eternal giver. I appreciate his kind heart, his brilliant marketing mind and most importantly, his friendship.

To the great folks at Killer Covers who enthusiastically take on projects for creation and always do a first class job. I love their enthusiasm for always delivering quality products.

At the risk of the acknowledgement section being longer than the content of the book ☺ please know that I am blessed with many more wonderful people in my life, including my enthusiastic personal assistant Lindsay Bouleau and the talented marketing genius Trace Haskins. I am grateful for your contribution to this book and my work. Thank you for all you do!

Introduction

MY HUSBAND AND I were married on July 25. A pastor married us in a beautiful outdoor ceremony. After Denis and I exchanged our vows, everyone held their breath as they waited for the magic words "I now pronounce you husband and wife, you may kiss the bride."

What did this pastor have—this power of being ordained and being able to declare a couple man and wife? Of course it's a legal system and we signed a legal document. But had anything really changed? Were we different beings? Wasn't I still the same Peggy I'd been five minutes ago and Denis still the same Denis?

Of course we were the same people! We were the same people but there was an understanding and a knowing. Denis and I had entered into a spiritual contract and that meant we were now husband and wife. We believed we were husband and wife, and because we believed, we became husband and wife. Other than a piece of paper, becoming husband and wife was just belief.

William James said, "Believe, and your belief will create the fact." It was belief that made us husband and wife. The pastor performed the religious ceremony, the government documents made it legal but it was our belief that married us.

What if I possessed a power similar to the pastor and could declare you a millionaire author and make it so? It just so happens that I do have that power. I have the power to declare you a millionaire author if you decide that is what you want. You must bring the belief.

In return for your belief, I am going to give you a promise: If you read this book carefully and follow through with the suggestions it contains, I know you will become a millionaire author, if that's what you truly desire. In fact, I declare you a millionaire author right now!

You have the right and the opportunity to claim your success; you can claim it right now! If you have something in your heart that you are passionate about sharing, make the decision that you are going to do it. Decide you are going to follow your passion and claim it by writing it on paper and carrying it around with you. Affirm it often, starting right now.

I decided to be a millionaire author long before any evidence of it manifested in my life. When I first proclaimed it to the universe, I felt very uncomfortable. But I knew I was passionate about bringing my message to the world and I knew that I wanted to impact people in a positive way and generate many millions of dollars in revenue.

You must make that decision too! It's vitally important to an author's success to be the person who is already successful; to feel what it feels like to be successful. You have to truly feel it! That's what I call the millionaire author mindset. I'm going to give you the very best tools for developing a millionaire mindset that I've gleaned from 14 years as a very successful author and more than three decades of studying personal development.

Introduction

I decided to become a millionaire author long before evidence of it ever manifested into my life. Like many people, I thought if I wrote a good book the buyers would come. I self-published my book *On Being the Creator of Your Destiny* and soon found myself with three thousand copies of a hardcover book on my dining room table and very few buyers. I knew that I had to take action if I wanted to be a successful author so I invested in attending a marketing program and one of the speakers at this event was a man named Jerry Jenkins who runs a company called The Jenkins Group.

Jerry walked out on stage and said, "If you're an author and you've written a book, five percent of your job is done." I remember thinking to myself "Hmmm, he must've said that wrong; five percent?" I felt like it had been a considerable amount of work to write the book. Then Jerry followed up by saying, "Ninety-five percent is the marketing."

That information has allowed me to help hundreds of clients land their book on the bestseller list as well as several of my own books. I often hear people say they aren't great writers. Guess what? You don't have to be! There are multiple ways to write a book and it can be really easy and fun. Part two of this book is about writing and marketing your book.

I teach courses on how to write your book and how to make it a best seller. There is a formula that you can use that will almost certainly guarantee your success. I can't possibly teach you the formula in one book, but I will share brilliant writing and marketing strategies that I know will ignite that burning desire inside you to become a millionaire author. Once you develop a burning desire and make the decision to become a millionaire author, you are well on your way.

That leads me to the third part that you will find later in the book, *The Millionaire Author: Making money*. How do you become a millionaire author? You turn your book into a moneymaking business. You turn your ideas, your expertise, your vision and what's in your heart into a revenue generating business that brings value to others.

It's not just about making money. It's about bringing value to the world and making a positive contribution to the lives of others. Let me say that again, because it is definitely worth repeating. Being a successful author or a millionaire author is not about the money. It's about bringing value to others that truly makes a positive contribution. It's about bringing the impression of increase to everyone you meet and having them want to invest in your programs, your coaching, your training seminars or whatever you decide to offer to the world. It follows the age-old premise that in order for you to receive you must first give.

There are many ways to generate six, seven, and eight figure incomes as an author. It's so important to recognize that this opportunity is available to anyone! Part three of this book is going to show you some of the countless ways you can convert your book and your story into the riches you desire.

The information in this book is enormously valuable and has the potential to catapult you into the life of your dreams as a successful author. Early in my career I heard a statistic that surprised me. It went like this: 93% of all books released will never sell more than 500 copies. This was a surprise at first, but even if it is true, it means there is an opportunity to be in that top 7% by learning and applying effective marketing practices for authors. This way, you too, can be in that top 7% of all authors.

Dr. Wayne Dyer says that it's not crowded along the extra mile. By reading this book, you are already part of that select group of people who are willing to go the extra mile. I wrote this book to save you thousands of dollars and years of wasted effort. It is my sincere wish that you become a millionaire author too. Use the information in this book to guide and inspire you to achieve your dreams as a successful author.

Part I
The Millionaire Mindset

CHAPTER 1

The Modern Day Gold Rush

THE OPPORTUNITIES FOR YOU as an author today are enormous beyond belief! Forbes created a list of the richest authors and for the first time in history, there is an author who has created a billion dollar net worth: J.K. Rowling. Rowling was the first, but there are many other authors who have generated hundreds of millions of dollars from doing what they love and sharing their creativity and talent with others.

If you do not know J.K. Rowling's story, you might assume that she was a literary genius from childhood and had all the financial support she needed. That is not the case for many successful authors and it certainly wasn't the case for J.K. Rowling. At one point, Rowling was a single mom with an infant daughter who was on social assistance. The story goes that she would take her daughter to a café and order an espresso or a coffee and sip it for a few hours to stay warm because she was unable to pay the heat bill for her apartment.

Rowling was unable to afford heat but she had an idea that came to her many years before, while she was travelling. It was an idea about a young boy who was a wizard. Rowling could not find a publisher for her book but she wrote *Harry*

Potter and the Philosopher's Stone anyway. After just three rejections, J.K. Rowling found a publisher and it became an instant success.

What causes a book to become an overnight success? It must be a well-written book that readers love so much that they recommend it to their friends. *Harry Potter and the Philosopher's Stone* was a great book that led to multiple books that were wildly successful. To date J.K. Rowling is the most successful author in history!

You can achieve the success you desire too! You might think that you cannot achieve this success because you are not as good a writer as J.K. Rowling. If you have an idea and can communicate, you can communicate your idea. If you can communicate your idea, you can definitely write a book. I am always grateful that God has blessed the world with editors but you'll read more about that in part two.

Consider E. L. James' *Fifty Shades of Grey* trilogy. James received harsh criticism for her writing and many people claimed the series was poorly written. E. L. James dreamed of writing a series of stories that readers would fall in love with and she was successful. *Fifty Shades of Grey*, *Fifty Shades Darker*, and *Fifty Shades Free* became the fastest selling books in history and it is widely known that in 2013 E. L. James earned ninety-five million dollars.

What about the books? How can books that are not perfectly written generate ninety-five million dollars? People loved the books and told their friends about them. Within days of each other, I had two of my friends tell me how much they loved the books.

The books might not have been perfectly written but the stories were definitely engaging. I purchased *Fifty Shades of Grey* to read on a flight from London to Toronto and I blushed a little when the flight attendant walked by and said, "Oh my goodness isn't that a wonderful book?" It may not have been a work of literary genius or something I would normally read, but it was fascinating and gripping. It was entertaining.

You might be asking about your non-fiction book. You can become a millionaire author regardless of your genre. Arthur Agatston created The South Beach diet and he self-published it as a pamphlet. He distributed hundreds of pamphlets of his South Beach Diet and it spread like wildfire! Within a year, he sold the rights to Rodale publishing house and sold seven million copies in the first year alone.

Why did *The South Beach Diet* become a runaway success? It was effective and people told their friends. *The South Beach Diet* has expanded into multiple versions including *The South Beach Diet Gluten Solution* and *The South Beach Diet Supercharge*. Agatston now sits at the head of a multi-million dollar empire.

You can enjoy the same success with your book. Were there other diet books on the market when Agatston released *The South Beach Diet?* Of course there were! But Agatston was really passionate about bringing his valuable knowledge to the world. He decided that he would step out and follow his passion.

What is your passion? What would you love to experience in your life? You absolutely can and should be a millionaire author if that is what you truly desire. Once you decide to become a millionaire and begin to work from that goal, you will begin to attract the people, the circumstances and whatever you need to make it happen no matter what challenges you might face.

No discussion of the modern day gold rush would be complete without mentioning the *Chicken Soup for the Soul* series by Jack Canfield and Mark Victor Hansen. My dear friend and mentor Bob Proctor participated in the million-dollar roundtable meeting with the authors where they first got the idea for the book and he told me about the meeting.

Like your book, *Chicken Soup for the Soul* started as an idea. One of the authors got an idea for a book of short stories written to inspire and lift the spirits of readers. When Jack Canfield and Mark Victor Hansen left the meeting, they didn't even have a title for the book. One of the two was inspired with the title in the middle of the night and called the other and said, "I've got the title! It's Chicken Soup or the Soul!" The response was "Okay great, now I can go back to sleep."

Today, Mark Victor Hansen and Jack Canfield hold The Guinness Book of World Records for the most successful book series. *Chicken Soup for the Soul* has more than 250 titles and has sold more than five hundred million copies worldwide. That's right: five hundred million books!

You can enjoy massive success as an author too, you really can! I want you to become a millionaire author, in fact, that's why I wrote this book.

I have generated multiple millions of dollars in profitable revenue, which is an extension of my books and I have seen many, many other authors achieve success. Many of these other millionaire authors have built a business around their passion, expertise and genre.

Consider the story of Selamwi who goes by the name Mawi Asgedom. When Asgedom was a young boy, he and his family fled from their native country of Ethiopia to Sudan escape the violence that was rampant in their village. Asgedom and his family lived in a refugee camp until they immigrated to the United States when he was seven. Asgedom family did not speak English fluently and relied on social assistance.

Despite such a tumultuous start in life, Mawi Asgedom refused to let his background or upbringing prevent him from achieving his goals. Asgedom graduated from Harvard University and enjoyed the honor of giving the commencement address at his convocation. In 2001 Asgedom sold the rights to his book *Of Beetles and Angles* and another self-help book for young readers to Little Brown publishing house for more than one hundred thousand dollars.

Today, Asgedom enjoys even greater success. Young audiences love his powerful and engaging motivational speaking and he has created a speaker-coaching business that is highly profitable. Asgedom turned his personal story of triumph in the face of extreme adversity in a business that allows him to bring great value to the world while living a wealthy and prosperous life.

Jim Everroad is another example of an individual who turned adversity into triumph when he lost his job as a high-school athletics coach. Everroad loved sports and was an athlete himself and he decided to convert his love of fitness into riches through sports writing.

Everroad had a technique for toning abs that he created and he decided to write a book called *How to Flatten Your Stomach*. Everroads sold more than two million copies of *How to Flatten Your Stomach* and went on to release many more books that became bestsellers. Like Asegdom, Everroad decided to turn adversity into opportunity.

Stephanie Dirks Ashcraft became a New York Times best-selling author and created a very successful series of cookbooks based on a college project where she wrote a book called *101 Things to Do with a Cake Mix*. I suspect if Dirks had told relatives or friends she thought she could become wealthy from her college project, they would have suggested she form a plan for the real world. But Dirks believed in herself and self-published *101 Things to Do with a Cake Mix*.

Despite being self-published with such an unusual title for her book, Dirks sold more than seven thousand copies of her book. This was very unusual and attracted the attention of a publisher in New York. The series that began as a college project has expanded into a very successful cookbook series. Like *Chicken Soup for the Soul*, Dirks series of *101 Things to Do with a Cake Mix* has expanded into many different titles.

Do you see the pattern here? There is no pattern! Any author can become a millionaire author. I have clients who ask if their book about holistic healing, or gardening, or Cajun cooking, or meditation, or whatever will sell. My answer is always the same, you can sell your book if there is an audience. As I have shown through these examples, there are millionaire authors who publish through a publishing house and there are those who self-published. There are millionaire authors who write novels and there are those who write non-fiction. You can become a millionaire author by writing a self-help or how-to type book. No matter what your genre and publishing choices, you can become a millionaire author.

One of the greatest rewards for me in my business is seeing my clients achieve success. It's what I love and it's why I keep doing what I do. If these and so many more authors can do it, so can you. You can have that luxury home. You can have that log cabin on the lake. You can drive that Porsche Carrera. You can generate multiple millions of dollars. You can have, do, or be anything you choose. If you want to be a millionaire author, you must simply develop the millionaire mindset and get on with the work. The modern day gold rush is on and it's up to you to stake your claim.

"REDUCE YOUR PLAN TO WRITING...THE MOMENT YOU COMPLETE THIS, YOU WILL HAVE DEFINITELY GIVEN CONCRETE FORM TO THE INTANGIBLE DESIRE."

~ NAPOLEON HILL

CHAPTER 2

Get Out of Your Own Way

I KNOW PEOPLE who have wanted to write a book for years! They have a message to share that they are really passionate about and they want to be successful. These people really want to make a positive contribution to the world but they're blocked. Sometimes they're blocked because they lack confidence in themselves or don't think their writing is effective. Sometimes they just don't believe they are worthy of success.

These would-be author millionaires just need to get out of their own way. If you want to become a millionaire author, you need to feel like a millionaire author. You must believe in your work more than anyone. If you experience doubt, you must kick it to the curb and let the garbage truck take it to the dump because it will only hold you back.

I remember when I first told my parents I was writing a book. Their response was, "You? You're writing a book? What could you possibly write a book about?" Don't get me wrong, I loved my parents very much and we had a really good relationship but that was their response. Were they trying to be funny? Or

Hurtful? No, they were not. My parents just did not think I was destined for a successful career as an author.

Thankfully, I had studied personal development for over fifteen years by that time and I knew I was capable of achieving any goal I set. Was it uncomfortable for me? Absolutely! Were there times when I was overcome with doubt? Definitely! But I moved forward despite the fears and misgivings and now my family and I reap the benefits.

Nothing is more important to me than my family. I am blessed to have a wonderful husband who I absolutely adore, my son who is the greatest gift life has ever given me, and now I have a grandson who brings me more joy than I imagined possible. My family is my number one priority.

When I wrote my first book, I was a single mom. It was very important to me create a wonderful life for my son. It was a lifelong dream for me to do what I love and be very successful. I wanted to make a positive contribution to the lives of millions of people doing meaningful worked that I loved and I wanted to generate millions of dollars in profitable revenue for my business.

I *decided* to become a successful author. I claimed to the universe that I, Peggy McColl, am a New York Times best-selling author and enjoy generating many millions of dollars in revenue for my profitable business. I acted like it was already real, I felt like it was already done, and I believed it was already my reality.

The most common question I am asked by my clients when I say that is, "How can you act, feel, and believe something that hasn't happened yet?" The answer is simple: you get out of your own way. Push your doubts and fears aside and step into the feeling! Just decide what you want to achieve and what it will feel like. When we were young children we played a game called "Make Believe". Make believe you are already successful. You've heard the term *act as if.* Act as if you have already achieved all of your goals.

Only you know what you would love and it is your responsibility to declare it to the universe. Invest some time getting really clear on your goal and write it down. The universe doesn't know your definition of a successful author therefore be specific about your outcome. What is important to you? What do you want to be recognized for? How are you now living your life now that you are a successful author? Are you the author of the number one New York Times best seller with a business that extends from the book and generates one hundred million dollars in profitable revenue? If that is something you want, you must claim it.

If I focused on the lack of belief of my parents or the people who reminded me that less than seven percent of authors sell more than five hundred copies, I would have moved away from my dream and never really lived the life I wanted. You must believe in yourself. You must believe in your work. You must know that you are worthy and deserving of abundance. You must decide what you want and go for it!

There are countless examples of other authors who decided on their outcome and achieved great success. Did they experience people in their lives telling them their idea was silly or reminding them they did not know how to write a book? Perhaps they did! But they believed in themselves and their dreams and persisted until they achieved the success they desired.

Amanda Hocking began writing when she was a little girl and dreamed of becoming a successful author. When her first two books did not sell, Hocking realized that she knew very little about the publishing industry and invested the time to learn about the book business.

When Hocking could not get an agent, she began to think of other ways to sell her books. Hocking saw the opportunity to reach massive numbers of readers when the sale of electronic and downloadable books exploded online. Hocking had her books formatted for Kindle and began selling them online.

Amanda Hocking was not an instant sensation like J.K. Rowling. When she began selling her books on Amazon, she had a full-time job that paid eighteen thousand dollars a year. Though she sold only small quantities of books when she first started selling online, Hocking kept writing and adding books to the virtual bookstores. Hocking earned her first million dollars when she was twenty-six and her second million by the time she was twenty-seven.

What did Amanda Hocking do that distinguished her from the countless others who do not become millionaire authors? She got out of her own way and did not allow fear to stop her. When her books were not selling, she made some changes. When she could not secure an agent, she found another way to bring her work out into the world. Amanda Hocking did not allow herself to be governed by feelings of doubt and fear.

One of the main reasons authors do not succeed is fear. In general, one of the main reasons people do not succeed is fear. Fear is debilitating. Many authors experience fear and doubt and those two emotions will kill dreams. Often, they are afraid to reach out to people who could help them bring their work to the world. Amanda Hocking did not allow such fear and doubt to prevent her success. Hocking found multiple ways to bring attention to her books. She found popular bloggers and posted on their sites, she reached out to people who were willing to review her books and she kept adding new titles online.

Amanda Hocking's success did not happen overnight, but it happened. Despite her lack of experience in the industry and her unsuccessful pursuit of an agent, Hocking had her dream and her persistence. The doubt, fear, and temporary rejection that authors often face did not prevent Hocking from becoming a millionaire author. Amanda Hocking's success is an excellent example of the power of believing in yourself and what your work can bring.

As an author, you must replace your fear with faith. Fear of failure prevents many excellent writers from becoming millionaire authors. When Richard Paul Evans wrote *The Christmas Box*, he asked his wife if she would read his manuscript. Evans gave his story to his wife and left the room to give her time to read. While his wife was reading, Evans could not contain his excitement and peeked into the room he had vacated. When Evans saw tears streaming down his wife's face, he was filled with self-doubt and fear. He thought, "Oh no! She hates my manuscript and is upset about having to break it to me."

As it turned out, Evans' wife was crying because the beauty of her husband's story had moved her to tears. She loved the story and begged him to share it with her sister who insisted on sharing the story with friends. Evans self-published *The Christmas Box* and began selling thousands of copies. Publishers began to approach Evans about buying rights to his story and he secured an agent who decided to auction the rights for *The Christmas Box*.

Simon and Shuster bought the rights to Richard Paul Evans' first story for more than four million dollars. In 1995 *The Christmas Box* became the first book to simultaneously reach the number one spot on the New York Times best sellers list in hard cover and soft cover edition and was made into a television movie. When a story elicits such a phenomenal response from the publishing industry, it is easy to assume the author must have known they'd written a winner. This was clearly not the case for Evans.

Evans' feelings of fear and self-doubt are common amongst authors and must be overcome if you want to become a successful author. One of the most famous and celebrated writers of all time, William Shakespeare said, "Our doubts are traitors and make us lose the good we oft might win by fearing to attempt." Do not allow your fear to govern your life and mar the success you deserve and want. If you really want to become a millionaire author, you must decide what you want, get out of your own way, and share your gift with the world.

"WHEN WE DO MORE THAN WE ARE PAID TO DO, EVENTUALLY WE WILL BE PAID MORE FOR WHAT WE DO."

~ ZIG ZIGLAR

CHAPTER 3

Dream with Your Eyes and Ears Open

"**ALL MEN DREAM,** but not equally. Those men who dream at night in the dusty recesses of their minds wake in the day and find that it was vanity; but the dreamers of the day are dangerous men, for they may act their dreams with open eyes to make it possible." —General George S. Patton

I first heard General Patton's famous dreamers quote in a Bob Proctor seminar many years ago. For some reason, it really resonated with me and led me to develop the most effective tool I have ever found for manifesting your desires. I call it your power life script. This technique harnesses your mind's power by combining visualization and repetition. I have been using my power life script for more than 20 years and it has helped me to manifest the amazing life of wealth and abundance that I am so grateful to provide for my family.

When I think about my life, before I stumbled into that first Bob Proctor seminar more than thirty-five years ago, I am always amazed by the difference between my childhood and youth and that of my son and grandson. The ripple effect from the success of my books and my business enabled me to create a life for my family that is abundant in every way. My son attended private school, we enjoyed first class vacations and our home is very comfortable. My son and grandson have always had a comfortable life.

My childhood was a little different. Our family home was eight hundred square feet with two bedrooms: one for my parents and one for the four kids to share. My brothers slept in bunk beds and my sister and I shared a small bed. My mom worked in a factory stuffing envelopes with junk mail and my dad managed a convenience store.

We had a summer cottage too but I cannot help but giggle when I think about the place we called our cottage. It was really just a room measuring about 8 x 20 square feet that my dad built on my grandmother's land. There was no electricity or plumbing. We cooked our dinner over a Coleman stove, we had campfires each and every night and yes, we did our business outside in the woods.

Those were leaner times but they were still magical. We did not have all the material things but we were still wealthy. I knew two things from a very young age: my family would always be my number one priority and I wanted to provide a comfortable home. I wanted the campfires and the laughter and the love that I enjoyed so much but I wanted to enjoy that experience in luxury.

I started working at the convenience store my dad managed when I was eight years old. He paid me to help stock the shelves and maintain the aisles. By the time I was twelve I was a seasoned worker and began summer employment at the factory where my mom worked.

By the time I got to high school, earning money was second nature to me. I worked in a grocery store in the evenings and attended high school during the day. I enjoyed earning money because I enjoyed the spending power. I loved being able to buy the trendy jeans whenever I wanted. I relished the feeling of having money to spend because it felt good.

After high school, I began working with computers. It was a natural fit for me. I'm not really a technical person but I love technology and I enjoy making it work. I worked full time during the day and I taught evening classes on word processing at local community colleges before the micro-computer was even in the market. It was during this time that I found my true passion.

I love to teach! Anybody who knows me knows that teaching is my absolute passion. When I taught at two community colleges in the evening, I was still technically a teenager and most of the students were women as old as my mom. I loved helping these women and I knew that I wanted to help people on a really big scale.

I knew what I wanted but I could not see how I was going to make it happen. That was when my company brought Bob Proctor and his teaching into my life and the rest, as they say, is history. From that very first day I met Bob Proctor, my life changed dramatically. I saw for the very first time that I was the one holding myself back.

When Bob said, "You can't escape from a prison if you don't know you're in one" it felt as though we were the only two people in the room and time stood still. That seminar changed my life forever. As I listened to Bob's words, I felt like the room was spinning. If what this man was telling me was real, then I was making a big mess of my life. I decided that day that I would study everything Bob Proctor wrote, recorded, and taught.

That was thirty-five years ago and I have not stopped studying personal development or following the advice of Bob Proctor. I have invested hundreds of thousands of dollars and countless hours travelling to and from personal development seminars and my investment has paid me great dividends. I would like to use some of the knowledge I took from my studies to save you time and money as you work towards becoming a millionaire author.

Unless you've been living under a rock for the last decade or so, you have heard about the power of visualization. You have probably heard stories about vision boards like the one John Assaraf shares in the hit movie "The Secret". John says that he was unpacking boxes in his new home and found some boxes that had been in storage for about five years. When Assaraf's five-year-old son asked what the boxes contained, Assaraf decided the easiest way to explain a vision board to his son would be to show him. Assaraf tells how he was overwhelmed with emotion when he saw the picture of the home that was posted on the five-year-old vision board because he realized the home they that they were moving into was the exact home displayed in the photo on the vision board.

Visualization is very powerful. I have been using visualization to manifest my desires for decades and it works. Before I wrote Your Destiny Switch, I decided it would be a New York Times best seller. It was uncomfortable at first because my nagging inner voice of doubt questioned if I was worthy of such a distinction and if could even write a New York Times best seller. I felt fear and doubt but I moved forward in spite of the fear and claimed my intention to the universe.

The day I received an advanced copy of the book jacket, I decided to harness my mind's power of visualization and use it to help me achieve my goal of making *Your Destiny Switch* a New York Times best seller. I went into my own book shelf and found a copy of Robert Kiyosaki's *Rich Dad Poor Dad* with the gold New York Times best-seller emblem on the cover. I cut the emblem from the cover of *Rich Dad Poor Dad* and taped it to the jacket of *Your Destiny Switch*. Then I made enough colored copies to place around my home and in my car.

As I gazed at *Your Destiny Switch*, complete with the New York Times best-seller emblem, I allowed myself to get excited about my goal. I would look at the image and get emotionally involved in the goal by imagining how it would feel when my book was on that list. *Your Destiny Switch* was a New York Times best-seller on the screen of my mind long before that distinction actually occurred.

You can and should harness your mind's power through visualization too. Wallace D Wattles talks about visualizing your goals in his book *The Science of Getting Rich*. Wattles said, "You must form a clear mental picture of what you want." You should be able to describe the image of your goal as if you were looking at a photograph. Remember, the universe does not know your definition of a successful author so you must be very specific about how this accomplishment will positively impact all areas of your life when you are setting your goal. If your goal is to earn a specific amount of money, try and visualize a day in your life after you have achieved your financial goal.

Back in the nineties, when I developed the technique I call your power life script which combines visualization with the first Law of learning: repetition. It's a process where you write a detailed description, similar to a manuscript of the life you really desire as if you were living that life already. The first step in the process is getting a clear image of how you would like to live.

Then you write your script out on paper. Describe your life in exquisite detail: Do you travel first class? How is your health? Is your family loving and supportive? Does your spouse surprise you with wonderful tokens of adoration? Is revenue pouring in? Are you blissfully happy? Answer these questions and script your life.

Write the description of every part of your life that is important to you and get excited about the life you are creating for yourself and your family. Write your script in positive terms and connect to the energy of your goal.

Now comes the fun part: take your script and record yourself reading about your ideal life as if you were experiencing it already. You do not need sophisticated recording equipment to record your power life script. You can use your phone or computer, or one of several free, downloadable software programs available online.

My power life script audio is less than thirty minutes long and I call it *My* Wonderful Life. I listen to it as often as I can. I play it when I am getting dressed for the day, I play it when I am driving to the store, I play it when I pick up my grandson and he listens to it with me. I play it often because it allows me connect with the feeling of experiencing my dream life. It's not enough for you to do the things you think will help you succeed as an author. If you want to be a successful, millionaire author, you must feel like a successful, millionaire author first.

Earl Nightingale could have been talking to a room full of authors when he said, "People think you earn a lot of money because you are successful. The truth is, you can only earn money after you are successful." You must feel it in your heart. You must believe you are the millionaire author you want to be before you can expect it to materialize.

You can become a millionaire author once you develop the millionaire mindset. There is more than enough of everything in the universe and you can choose the life you want to live.

Developing a millionaire mindset is simple, it isn't necessarily easy, but it is very simple.

You must believe in yourself, your work, and your goals. You must act and feel like a millionaire author and most importantly, you must be persistent. Push fear and doubt out the door and roll out the red carpet for faith. When you know and believe you are a millionaire author, the manifestation of your belief is imminent.

"THREE RULES OF WORK: 1. OUT OF CLUTTER FIND SIMPLICITY; 2. FROM DISCORD FIND HARMONY; 3. IN THE MIDDLE OF DIFFICULTY LIES OPPORTUNITY."

~ ALBERT EINSTEIN

Part II
Writing and Marketing

CHAPTER 4

So You Think You Can't Write

SO MANY LIFE-CHANGING STORIES remain untold because people doubt their ability to write a good book. Do not let this happen to you. Make the decision to bring your message to the world knowing that you can write your book with ease regardless of your writing ability, your genre or whether you are writing fiction or non-fiction. I know this because I have written many best-selling books and I do not consider myself a particularly good writer.

You are probably asking yourself, "What the heck does she mean she's not a good writer? She's a New York Times best-selling author!" Success as an author does not necessarily mean that an author is an exceptionally gifted writer. If you have a great idea for a book you can write a great book with the help of a great team, regardless of your writing ability.

There are multiple ways to write a book. If you are a speaker, you can have your presentation recorded, transcribed, and edited into a book. You can hire a ghostwriter to bring your message to the world. You can repurpose articles and blog posts you have already written. You can teach a course and have it transcribed. There are many different ways to write a book. Let me tell you how I wrote *The Millionaire Author*.

My years of coaching and teaching have taught me that people are more likely to make a buying decision based on something they want rather than something they need. Does an author need to be successful? No, but they sure wants to succeed. Does an author need to be a millionaire? No, but I imagine that is your reason for reading this book. I always try to give people what they want and give them the most value for their investment. That is how *The Millionaire Author* was born.

Most of my clients sign up for multiple programs offered on my website. I teach courses on everything from how to write your book in a weekend to how to grow a multi-million dollar online business. I noticed that many of my author clients wanted an all-inclusive course to give them tips for writing and marketing their books and then showed them how to turn their book into a million dollar business. What author doesn't want to be a millionaire author?

I got the idea for an online program that would show the necessary steps to creating the seven figure income people desired. As you will read in chapter five, you must be willing to distinguish yourself from others if you want success in your business. I was so sure people would find great value in *The Millionaire Author* that I offered free registration for the six hour program with the option of investing and a choice for the amount they would invest after it was delivered.

When I told some of my peers what I was planning to do, they were shocked. They loved the idea of *The Millionaire Author* but questioned my plan to give it away, "Why are you just giving away an entire program Peggy?" was the question I was repeatedly asked. When I explained my plan for giving people the choice of whether to invest in the program, they were impressed that I had found such a creative way to distinguish my program.

I got the idea for *The Millionaire Author* on a Sunday and I taught the program five days later. Remember, the Universe loves speed and if you give yourself a deadline, you will attract everything you need to accomplish your goal. The response was enormous and it was a marvelous event. I had people from South Africa, Australia, New Zealand, Japan, England, Ireland, China, and all over North America join the event. Hundreds of people registered and many of them invested in the material. Since I record every program I teach as a potential future offering on my website, I had more than six hours of valuable content at my disposal. People loved *The Millionaire Author* and begged me to write this book.

You might remember at the beginning of this chapter I said that I do not consider myself an exceptionally good writer. I enjoy writing but teaching is my true passion. Since I taught and recorded the material for the program, I simply had it transcribed and edited to create the content for the book you are reading now.

Can you do something like this? Of course you can. If you can teach your program, you can create a book. If you can have a conversation with another person, you can create a book. This is just one of the multiple ways you can write your book. I teach a course where I cover the process of writing your book step by step. If you are interested in learning more about this program, please visit my website: http://PeggyMcColl.com.

By this point, I suspect you are either ready to start writing, recording, or teaching your material. If you still have concerns about the actual writing of your book, or simply do not want to write your book, fear not because there are other options. There are many different levels of support available to you as an author. When I think or say the word editor, the first thought that pops into my mind is, "Thank you God for putting good editors on this planet." I am more than happy to give credit for the readability of my books to good editing and ghostwriters.

Most authors understand the editing process but many are unsure about ghostwriters. Ghostwriters act as a writing partner with the author. A common misconception is that ghostwriters write the book and the author adds their name. Although part of that statement may be true, most books are created from the author's idea, experience, knowledge and expertise.

Gay and Katie Hendricks are a married team who specialize in helping people enjoy more meaningful and fulfilling relationships. Gay Hendricks has published more than thirty books, several of which are co-authored by Katie.

A few years ago, Gay had a great idea for a novel and he hired a professional novelist to finish the product. Hendricks wrote the story initially and then turned it over to his ghostwriter. When the ghostwriter finished, the professional editor made it even better. The team improved Hendricks' masterpiece. Who wrote the book? Gay Hendricks.

I have used ghostwriters on several occasions and have had amazing results. Not only did I know exactly what I wanted to share, I was a big part of the process. A ghostwriter will get to know your voice and your message. You provide the story and the message, the ghostwriter assembles it into a package that's ready for the editor.

Regardless of how you get your book completed, it is important to find the inspiration to complete your book.

I would like to address the next question you might be asking right now, "I don't have a publisher, what now?" The second most common reason authors refrain from bringing their message to the world is difficulty finding a publisher. Many of my clients are first-time authors without an agent or publisher. Publishers are great if you have one. They will format and print your book and you will be a published author.

You will also be a published author if you self-publish. Print-on-demand has made self-publishing the easy choice for many first-time authors. Without a platform and a large following, many publishing houses are just not interested in new authors. Self-publishing is relatively inexpensive and the fastest way to bring your message to the world. Some people think that self-published books will not achieve the distinction of best sellers. This is simply not the case. Many of the most widely successful books of all time were self-published.

James Redfield self-published *The Celestine Prophecy* in 1992 and sold eighty thousand copies from the trunk of his car. In 1994, Warner Books bought the rights to his book and it went on to sell more than twenty million copies and stayed on the New York Times best-seller list for three years. *The Celestine Prophecy* led to a very successful sequel and made James Redfield a very wealthy man and a source of inspiration for authors everywhere.

You might recall chapter one of this book where I discuss E. l. James' wildly successful *Fifty Shades of Grey* trilogy that one year resulted in a ninety-five million dollar annual income for the author. Did you know the story was originally self-published with another title? It was originally posted online as *Master of the Universe* and was picked up by an Australian publishing house. If you are think that self-published authors cannot enjoy eight figure incomes, think again.

E. L. James books are a great example of the importance of your book's title. You want to pick a great title that readers will remember. Your title does not have to be something that will make people say, "Wow, that's a great title!" There was a very successful series of children's books called *The Adventures of Captain Underpants*. Do you think people heard that title and thought, "Great title, I have to read that book"? Probably not.

Your title must be memorable. *The Adventures of Captain Underpants* is a tough title to forget. *Who Moved My Cheese?* is another book that sold tens of thousands of copies. Was the title profoundly moving? No, but it was intriguing. There are many examples of published books that went from almost no sales to selling millions of copies by changing the title.

I have been blessed to know and study with some of the world's greatest motivational speakers including the late Zig Ziglar. Ziglar was a wonderful person, an incredible speaker, and a great storyteller who wrote a book. Ziglar's book contained many stories, but there were three particular stories that taught valuable lessons. He released his book *Biscuits, Fleas and Pump Handles* without much success. Ziglar knew his book was a winner, so he decided to change the title to *See You at the Top*. Ziglar sold millions of copies of *See You at the Top* and launched his career to astonishing new heights.

What else do you need to get started? Pick an amazing title, set a deadline to complete your book, and start writing. You can do this. I sometimes feel that my books are almost like children to me. Each one is special but I cannot pick a favorite. My books are one of the vessels through which I am fulfilling my life's purpose by making a positive contribution to people all over the world.

"YOU CAN HAVE EVERYTHING IN LIFE YOU WANT IF YOU'LL JUST HELP ENOUGH OTHER PEOPLE TO GET WHAT THEY WANT!"

~ ZIG ZIGLAR

CHAPTER 5

Dare to Bake Cookies

I WROTE MY FIRST BOOK *On Being the Creator of Your Destiny* because I like to follow my friend and mentor Bob Proctor's advice and reduce things down to the ridiculous. There were a lot of complicated and preachy self-help books on the market and far too few that distilled things down to the most basic level so that anybody could understand the content. I was passionate about bringing my message to the world and I was excited about the lives I would change. Like many authors, I thought if I wrote a great book, readers would come.

A short while later, I found myself with three thousand hardcover copies of my book in my dining room and no buyers.

Early in my author career I invested in learning, understanding and applying proven book-marketing skills. As a result I have created a system for making any book a best seller, when followed. The wonderful thing about the system is that it is repeatable and as a result, I've made many of my own books international bestsellers and helped my clients accomplish the same.

And, now in my career I primarily work with authors; published authors and self-published authors.

Print-on-demand publishing has made it very easy to self-publish a book. You can publish through CreateSpace on Amazon.com for free if you can design your cover and edit your own work. Even with a team, self-publishing is relatively inexpensive. Since the introduction of print-on-demand technology, there has been an explosion in the number of books published every year. The market is saturated with authors from every genre trying to bring their message to the world in a big way. How do you make yourself stand out from the crowd? You do something that distinguishes you from everyone else.

Since the key to a successful launch is to engage others to support your book launch, you must do something to make these potential partners notice and want to support your campaign. People with very large email lists are likely seasoned online marketers who are familiar with joint ventures and are very selective about the people with whom they partner. You must do something to bring attention to yourself and your book or you run the risk of getting lost in an ocean of authors.

A successful launch requires time, effort, and persistence but the rewards can be tremendous. Let's look at an example of a client of mine who distinguished herself through a little effort and creativity and sold the rights to her book for more than two million dollars.

When Elle Newmark was in her late fifties, she decided she wanted to find a publisher for her book *The Bones of the Dead*. Newmark first tried to get an agent to secure a publishing deal for her book, but after two agents and no contract, she was frustrated and decided to self-publish her work. Much like me when I published my first book, Newmark found herself with a great book that was not selling so she decided that she needed to learn about marketing.

Elle Newmark decided to invest in my program and launch her book through a bestseller campaign. Elle studied my program and realized that the way to a successful launch was finding partners with big email lists who would support her campaign. Here is where Elle Newmark became one of the few authors who were willing to go the extra mile. Newmark was determined to stand out from the crowd and she did so very successfully.

Since her book was called *The Bones of the Dead*, Newmark spent a day baking twelve dozen cookies in the shape of dog bones. Elle then packaged the cookies in twelve beautiful gift baskets and sent them to people she wanted to support her book launch. I received one of those twelve baskets and it certainly got my attention. Elle got the support she sought for her launch by distinguishing herself from the crowd.

But Elle Newmark did not stop there. The day before her book launch, Newmark personally emailed four hundred agents and publishers introducing herself and her book. Newmark simply said, "Tomorrow I am doing a virtual book launch for my self-published novel *The Bones of the Dead*. Watch it on Amazon.com because you are going to see it rise up the charts to become a bestseller. I am looking for a publisher for this book. If you are interested, please contact me within the next twenty-four hours." Within twenty-four hours, she had more than a dozen offers from agents and publishers.

When I share that story with clients, the response is often, "Four hundred emails? That seems like a lot of work!" It was certainly more effort than most people put into their campaigns but I do not think it took her very much time. Each email was personalized, but the body of the email was simply cut and pasted.

After signing with an agent from the William Morris Agency, Newmark's book went for auction. I was so thrilled when I received a message in my inbox with the subject: Are you sitting down? I opened the email from Elle and she announced that Simon and Shuster preempted all other bids and bought the rights to *The Bones of the Dead* for more than two million dollars.

Elle Newmark was not a technical person nor did she have experience in online marketing. What did Elle Newmark have that so many authors do not? Why was she so successful? Because she dared to be creative and stand out. Without a platform or email list, which you will read more about in the next chapter, she showed publishers that she was willing to market her book.

By reading this book and following through with the suggestions it contains, you may also find yourself on the road less travelled and you can also reap the rewards like Elle Newmark. Becoming a millionaire author is an opportunity that is available to anyone who is willing to go the extra mile.

There are so many ways to market your book, but the bottom line is always the same. If you want your book to sell, you must create the buzz. Before you can harness the power of word-of-mouth, you must have people reading your book. How do you get people to want to read your book? You must create a demand.

Back in the sixties, a woman named Jacqueline Susann wrote the manuscript for her novel *Valley of the Dolls*. It was a fascinating novel about narcotics and the party lifestyle that accompanied them. The manuscript was rejected many times and when Susann finally secured a publisher, she created a demand for *Valley of the Dolls* in a very unconventional way.

Instead of launching her book and encouraging as many people as possible to buy when *Valley of the Dolls* was released, Susann drove around the country buying all the copies of her book. Susann created the demand for her book by making it unavailable. *Valley of the Dolls* sold more than thirty million copies.

Much like the *Fifty Shades of Grey* trilogy, *Valley of the Dolls* was criticized and people claimed that Jacqueline Susann was not a very good writer. Regardless of the quality of writing, people obviously loved the story. The critics seem to think that a book must be perfectly written to be successful. I don't know about you but I would call a book that sells thirty million copies a very definite success.

When you analyze the stories behind many of the most successful books in history, you will find that most of the authors did things that other authors were not willing to do. If you really want to be a millionaire author, you must be willing to go the extra mile.

A Canadian named David Chilton wrote and self-published a book called *The Wealthy Barber*. It was a fable where a man receives financial advice from his barber during his haircuts. Chilton decided to become a great speaker and spent his days doing interviews and travelling the country giving presentations. Did this require effort and sacrifice? Absolutely! Was it worth the effort? I believe so. *The Wealthy Barber* sold more than one million copies in Canada alone and went on to be the biggest seller in Canadian history, second only to the Bible.

Though we discussed Jack Canfield and Mark Victor Hansen earlier in this book, their strategy for making their *Chicken Soup for the Soul* series such a huge success is worth mentioning here. They set their goal of selling one-and-a-half million copies in eighteen months—then they got on with the work.

Canfield and Hansen decided that they would do five things every day to promote their book. This might not sound difficult but I do not know many authors would be willing to commit to the same plan. I heard Canfield tell the story about how creative they had to be to find five things to promote their book each day. He says he was struggling to think of the fifth promotional idea for a day during the O. J. Simpson trial when he had an amazing idea that led to more exposure than they could have imagined.

The O. J. Simpson case was a media-frenzy from the start. Millions of people watched police pursue the American football player in his white Ford Bronco for hours. There was unprecedented media access to the trial and many millions of viewers watched the trial from their homes. The judge ordered that the jury be sequestered for the duration of the trial to prevent influence from the media. Canfield got the idea to send the jury copies of *Chicken Soup for the Soul* and took action. The day after he sent the books, the twelve jury-members and two alternates walked into the courtroom carrying a copy of *Chicken Soup for the Soul*.

Was that the reason for the overwhelming success of the *Chicken Soup for the Soul* series? Who knows? I cannot say for certain but I know that exposing your books to many millions of people is good marketing.

Good marketing does not have to be difficult or costly. You must be willing to do things that others will not and you must make yourself stand out. Do you have to be massively unique and completely different from other authors? No, you just need to do what it takes to be noticed.

I have many clients whose self-doubt makes them wary about stepping out and distinguishing themselves but I always remind them that ninety-five percent of an author's job is marketing. You must step out and be noticed. The key to marketing your book is simple: Dare to be creatively different. Stand out, be noticed, and do what other authors are not willing to do. Dare to bake cookies.

"ANYBODY CAN WISH FOR RICHES, AND MOST PEOPLE DO, BUT ONLY A FEW KNOW THAT A DEFINITE PLAN, PLUS A BURNING DESIRE FOR WEALTH, ARE THE ONLY DEPENDABLE MEANS OF ACCUMULATING WEALTH."

~ NAPOLEON HILL

CHAPTER 6

Reach Out and Touch Everyone

DID YOU HEAR a little voice singing, "Reach out and touch someone?", when you read the title of this chapter? You are not alone if you did. That catchy little jingle from AT&T's Twenty Million Voices campaign plays in my mind when I read this section and it makes me feel a little nostalgic when I think back to life before the Internet arrived on the scene.

AT&T's jingle was the most effective campaign in the company's history. It was created in 1979 by an advertising agency called N. W. Ayer and Son to increase the company's popularity and generate more long distance customers. It is an excellent example of effective advertising since it is easily identifiable decades later.

You are probably asking yourself why I am telling you about AT&T's advertising from the seventies. That four second jingle is more than effective advertising. It is a reminder of how far technology has progressed and how much greater the opportunities are for you as an author today.

With more than two-and-a-half billion people online and over two hundred million websites, you really can reach out and touch almost everyone. Becoming a millionaire author has never been easier and I want to share the single, most important strategy for building an online empire that generates multiple millions of dollars in revenue: build an email list.

Whenever I see a website without an opt-in form or a sign-up link, I think, "Wow, they're really missing the boat." Growing your email list will help you launch your book to bestseller status. Growing your list will help you attract support from seasoned online marketers with substantial email lists themselves. Growing your list will help you build a platform. Did I mention you have the potential to generate millions of dollars by offering yours or other people's valuable products and services to your email list?

You will read more about affiliate marketing in part three of this book but since you are probably reading this book with the intention of using the ideas it conveys to create your own multi-million dollar business, it's important to know that list-building has enormous revenue-generating potential even if you do not have your own products and services to sell.

While creativity is important to your success as an author and entrepreneur, you do not have to reinvent the wheel to grow your email list. There are countless ways to build your list and dozens of models to follow that will help you grow your list in record time with ease.

The best way to build your list is by giving something of value away. As my dear friend Bob Proctor always says, "You cannot give too much away." On the front page of your website, you must have something to give away to entice people to share their contact information. Your freebie must be benefit-oriented and extremely valuable to people. You really want to leave your new subscribers with the impression of "increase".

What kinds of gifts can you offer to build your list? There are too many to name, but here are just a few suggestions that are easy, fun, and inexpensive. You might want to write a downloadable tip sheet or special report or create a downloadable audio recording that is rich with content and useful tips. You might create a daily inspirational message for your list. Think of something you can create that will be really valuable to your subscribers.

I am constantly thinking about new and exciting ways to bring value to my list and ways to increase its size. When I think about creating a product to give away, I ask myself, "What do people really want? What are they hungry for?" Every product I create is designed to bring enormous value while answering the demands of the market. It is my purpose to make a positive contribution to the lives of millions and I create my products and offerings with integrity and the spirit of service.

One of my best-seller program graduates is also incredibly authentic and passionate about enriching the world is a lovely woman by the name of Jennifer McLean. I met Jennifer after she wrote *The Big Book of You* and invested in my bestseller program. Energy healing is McLean's passion and she is really enthusiastic about bringing her message to the world. When Jennifer decided she wanted to extend beyond her book, she wanted something that would bring the world's leading experts on energy healing to millions of people so she created a free tele-summit and called it "Healing With the Masters."

McLean interviews experts in the area of energy healing and offers free access to people who register. Registration is free and often the experts will create and make an offer that is exponential in value and an inexpensive investment. The interviews give enormous value to people who register and revenue from sales gets divided between the expert and McLean.

How did McLean put it all together? First, she identified a number of experts in the industry that she wanted to interview. I was one of the experts for her series and it was incredibly beneficial for both of us. What's interesting about experts is that they generally love doing interviews and will gladly agree to them.

McLean contacted numerous authors and recognized experts in the field of energy healing and asked if she could interview them. The experts agreed to send emails to their list promoting the event and to create a product they could sell and share the revenue with her. Each expert sent emails to their lists and McLean's list size grew exponentially and she generated revenue for her business when people decided to purchase the expert's offering.

"Healing With the Masters" has been growing for many years and has generated millions of dollars in revenue. The value "Healing With the Masters" brings to the world is immeasurable and enjoys making a positive impact on hundreds of thousands of people.

McLean's model is a wonderful model to replicate because it is an example of how easy, fulfilling, and lucrative a single idea can be.

Many seasoned online marketers have multiple websites whose sole purpose is to grow their email lists. There are many different possibilities for capturing contact information that are easy to use and relatively inexpensive. I use an email list service and there are many excellent choices. All you need to create a list-building website is a list service and a downloadable product or service to give away.

I have clients who send inspirational messages and stories to their list of subscribers. Bob Proctor's "Insight of the Day" site is an example of a site that generates millions of dollars in profitable revenue by sending inspirational quotes and stories to subscribers and offering them exclusive savings on products and services they promote.

Bob Proctor's son Brian thought of creating Insight of the Day in 2000 and it has been a tremendous success. Insight of the Day has a substantial subscriber base and generates healthy revenue by offering valuable products and services that are attractive to their subscribers at an exclusive discount. Should Brian Proctor decide to sell the website, there would be people lining up to purchase for millions of dollars.

These are just two simple, inexpensive, and easy ways to build your email list. You can learn from these models to create your own list building site or event. It really does not matter what service you are bringing to the world as long as it is valuable to subscribers and it comes from a place of authenticity.

You must be true to the embodiment of your message. If you are claiming to be an expert on vegan cooking, you had better be an amazing vegan chef yourself. If you plan to teach people how to create wealth in a specific industry, you must have already done so yourself. If your life is not congruent with your message, you will run into obstacle after obstacle and you will mar your chances for success. Be certain that your message is an authentic part of you.

I am blessed to serve hundreds of clients and bring my message to millions of people. I help authors write their books and make them best sellers and I help them expand beyond their book and turn their ideas into revenue generating businesses or I give them ideas to turn their passion into profit. I have the right to teach this material because I have applied it in my own life and turned my own books into bestsellers that generate millions of dollars in profitable revenue. I continuously study the material I am sharing in *The Millionaire Author* and my business just keeps expanding.

Whether you are an online marketing expert or an author-to-be trying to build a business, you must bring value and enrich the lives of others. Everything from an email to a website carries energy and you must commit to leave everyone you connect with through your writing, your marketing, your audiences, your coaching clients, your students, and whomever else you meet, with the impression of increase. When you focus your efforts on enriching the lives of others in everything you do, the astonishing Law of Compensation guarantees you will be rewarded.

"IF A MAN EMPTIES HIS PURSE INTO HIS HEAD, NO ONE CAN TAKE IT AWAY FROM HIM. AN INVESTMENT OF KNOWLEDGE ALWAYS PAYS THE BEST INTEREST."

~ BENJAMIN FRANKLIN

Part III
Cash is King

CHAPTER 7

Unlimited Possibilities

THIS IS THE PART of my business that makes me really excited. I love, love, love teaching people how to turn their books and/or ideas into money-making machines. There are so many ways to turn your book and/or ideas into millions of dollars in profitable revenue. I'll bet you already had an idea or two about how you can open the floodgates to prosperity. *The Millionaire Author* was an idea that is now generating revenue in my business and it was inexpensive, easy, and an absolute pleasure to create. You can create your own lucrative products and services just as easily. There are unlimited possibilities.

If you are like me and like to jump to the part about earning money, you should turn back and read chapter one: "The Modern Day Gold Rush." You will read about authors like J. K. Rowlings, E. L. James, and Jack Canfield and Mark Victor Hansen whose books sold millions of copies and earned them hundreds of millions of dollars. The stories of overnight success and runaway self-published books are inspiring. They show you what is possible. It's possible for you too.

There's great news for you if your book does not sell millions of copies or spend years on The New York Times Best-Seller

List. There are countless ways to extend beyond your book and turn your book into a multi-million dollar revenue generator. Most millionaire authors earn their revenue from sources other than their book. In some cases, authors become millionaires without ever selling a copy of their books.

A corporate consultant named Carol Abramson decided to write Not 3 but 21: *The Investor Relations Audience Every Public Company's CEO Must Understand* and gave it to potential clients. Out of the 250 copies Abramson gave away, 100 of those who received the book became clients who generated more than two million dollars in consulting fees.

Many experts hesitate to share their knowledge in a book that costs twenty dollars because they think people will not invest in their other services. In most cases, the exact opposite is true. When you write a book and demonstrate a really good understanding of a specific area, it's an instant credibility builder. You are perceived to be an expert in your field and people will want more of your products and services. You can write a book to create demand for your services.

If you have something to teach, you can easily generate revenue online and offline. I run my business, Dynamic Destinies, from my home. My business is primarily online and I run it from my laptop. I do not have a large staff of printers, editors, and assistants. In fact, aside from my one assistant, all of the people who work for me are contract employees. I have very little overhead for my corporation. Though I travel for speaking engagements that also generate revenue for my business, I run my business from home.

What are some of the products and services I've created as an extension of my books? I've created eCourses (webinars, teleseminars) and downloadable programs, audio recordings and flash drives, and workbooks and guidebooks. I teach courses that I record and sell on my site, I offer coaching and mentoring and I do speaking engagements where I sell products and services from the stage. I always have multiple products and services available and I constantly pay attention to the needs and wants of my clients.

You can create your own products like these to extend beyond your book too. You can generate income from teaching and recording a course. You can then sell the downloadable version on your website as a source of passive income. You will read more about the benefits of creating passive income in the next chapter but it is definitely important enough to your accumulation of wealth to be mentioned several times throughout this book.

You read about Jennifer McLean who enjoys success hosting her "Healing With the Masters" tele-summit. That opportunity is available for you too. Another client who I had the pleasure of serving is Marie Forleo. Like McLean, Marie Forleo earns millions of dollars in revenue from expanding beyond her book.

Marie Forleo knew from the time she was in her early twenties that she wanted to do work that was meaningful for her and helpful for women. After starting a coaching business, she wrote her book *How to Make Every Man Want You and Every Woman Want to Be You*.

From the moment I met Marie Forleo I just knew she was one of those people who was going to achieve great things in her life. Forleo was confident, dedicated, knowledgeable, persistent, and very attractive and enthusiastic. Forleo launched her career through effective use of the marketing techniques she learned from my bestseller program.

Success was not instant for Forleo. After launching programs and other services, she began hosting retreats for women. Marie Forleo ran a program for entrepreneurs program and does much the same work as I do, helping entrepreneurs build their business and improve their lives. Since she is exceptionally good at speaking and recording video, she runs an online service called Marie TV. Marie Forleo has built her business from her book and her annual revenue is in the seven figures.

What was behind Marie Forleo's success? Forleo knew she had something valuable to share, she listened to what her clients wanted and she created quality offerings based on those wants. Marie is also confident. You will see a common characteristic of successful people when you notice they all have confidence.

Are you starting to see other success patterns here? Most millionaire authors do much the same thing. Millionaire authors find and respond to the demand for services and products, then create multiple products to meet that demand. When you really tune into the pulse of your market, ideas for generating revenue beyond your book will begin to flash through your mind. It's up to you to decide how many ideas to turn into products and offerings.

I have a year-long mentoring program called the All Access Pass. Like my other products and services, I created this program to meet the demands of the market. I had several programs of shorter durations that involved one-on-one coaching and many of my clients would join multiple programs. After several clients expressed the desire to have access to all my programs and one-on-one coaching for an entire year, I responded by creating the All Access Pass.

One of the first things I do with a new client is show them how to create a revenue model for their business. I will not spend much time telling you what not to do, but it is important that you run your author business just like any other business. You must consider where you are investing your money to ensure maximum return. I know numerous authors who spent considerable amounts of money on publicity without generating revenue for their business.

Another author I know was invited to appear on Good Morning America. The author flew her family to New York City and rented a suite at The Plaza Hotel. Though she made a wonderful appearance on the show, there was almost no increase in book sales and she was very disappointed. You must pay attention to the bottom line and be flexible. If people are not responding to a new product or services you must be willing to adapt and create a new offering that meets demand.

There are unlimited possibilities for you to extend beyond your book and build a multi-million dollar revenue generating business. Creativity, good marketing, and quality products that bring value to your clients will get you on your way to becoming a millionaire author.

There has never been a better time to be an author. Technology has made brining your message to the world easy and inexpensive and the world is more accessible than it has ever been. The opportunities to be a millionaire author really are unlimited. There are over two-and-a-half billion people and more than one-and-a-half trillion dollars being spend through e-commerce. You can claim your millionaire status right now and if you follow the suggestions in this book and model the examples I share, you will be on your way to achieving the life you desire.

"WHEN I WAS YOUNG, I THOUGHT MONEY WAS THE MOST IMPORTANT THING IN LIFE. NOW THAT I'M OLD—I KNOW IT IS."

~ OSCAR WILDE

CHAPTER 8

Earn Money in Your Sleep

YOU CAN AND SHOULD earn millions of dollars doing what you love. It isn't enough to simply find your passion. You must discover your passion, recognize where the desires are in the industry, fulfill those desires better than anyone else and pay attention to what is working and what is not.

When you harness the technique I will teach in this chapter, you will soon realize that you really can create the life of your dreams where you live in abundance and do what you love.

Do you know that only three percent of people earn ninety-seven percent of all the money that is earned? These people have learned how to generate Multiple Sources of Income (MSI) to become wealthy.

More than ninety percent of the money-earning population trade their time for wages. The trouble with this way of earning money is that you will eventually run out of time. I was asked just before I delivered *The Millionaire Author* program how many sources of income I had and what they were. I did not know the answer. I receive checks in the mail for royalties for my books and online money transfers for affiliate marketing. I have an app out there in the world that I receive royalties for and I have many downloadable programs available for purchase from my website. My books have been translated into numerous foreign languages and I receive royalties from the foreign rights publishing houses. Money is always flowing into my business and in many cases, the work is complete and the product is downloadable.

These great examples of passive income are available to you too. I would love for you to model multiple sources of revenue and generate revenue in your business. I created *The Millionaire Author* with you in mind and it would bring me great pleasure to hear of the lucrative sources of income you have created for your business based on the knowledge you took from this book.

I have a client who has a completely automated website with downloadable audio recordings available for purchase. The recordings are already finished and the shopping cart takes care of the sale. Her website is earning money 24 hours a day and she does not have to even be there.

You're probably asking how you can set up multiple sources of income and earn money while you sleep. I mentioned several ways for you to consider. Royalties from your book and foreign rights publishing are one source of passive income. Teach and record a program that you can sell and deliver electronically (whether you are there or not). Host a free tele-summit or webinar series and sell the recording. There are so many possibilities. Between passive income and multiple sources of income, you can create a very lucrative business that does not require much of your time. This frees more of your time to do what you love.

Another idea for creating an source of income is to record a program you deliver and offer the course as a downloadable program from your website. You can even have the content of your program transcribed and edited and then you have another book to sell. How many sources of income should you have? As many sources as you want.

You do not have to create all your programs and services at the same time. Get one product or service running smoothly before moving on to the next. Bob Proctor tells a story about a performer who was spinning eighteen plates at the top of long sticks. The performer would race along and keep them spinning. Just when it looked as though one might fall, the performer would get it going again. Bob says it was phenomenal to think of the concentration of the performer.

After the performer finished and was chatting with the audience, Bob said someone asks the man how he could possibly get and keep those plates spinning at the same time. The performer replied that it was easy, he just started with one plate and got it spinning really well before he moved on to the next plate.

You can use this method too. Rather than creating half a dozen new products, create one and make sure it is established and running smoothly, then when you are ready, simply create another source of revenue, like a downloadable audio program. Then you add a third, and a forth, and a fifth. You are much more likely to succeed if you focus your energy on getting your first product or service running really well before you move on to others.

Affiliate marketing is another opportunity for a source of income. Affiliate marketing is where you promote other people's product to your list and you receive compensation for each of your list member that purchased. There are countless ways to use affiliate marketing to your advantage. Not only can you make money selling other people's products and services. Affiliate marketing is used for launching virtually everything online.

I have friends who have generated millions of dollars by promoting other people's products and services to their list. As we discussed in chapter six, Reach Out and Touch Everyone, growing a list can be fun, inexpensive, and fast. If affiliate marketing is of interest to you, you should definitely focus on investing the time to grow your eMail list.

You should also be thinking about establishing future sources of income. Do you have a unique method of doing something that you can teach? If you can teach it, so can other people and you might think of creating a certification program. People could invest money to train with you and teach your method and you would be compensated for your name or brand. Revenue flowing into your business is the goal.

There is a fascinating example of an idea that grew into an entire business of multiple sources of income. Nancy Martin loved quilting and decided that she wanted to write multiple books on quilting. Martin started her own self-publishing company and called it The Patchwork Place. Within a relatively short time, she renamed the company Martingale and Company and she ended up publishing more than four hundred titles and selling over twelve million books. Nancy Martin wrote forty books on quilting many of which went on to be the bestselling books in the company.

Who would have thought one lady could build a publishing empire that netted her a fortune based on her love of quilting? It just goes to show that it really does not matter what your passion is, when you connect with it on a deeper level, the way to build the business will come to you.

If you do not have multiple sources of income in your life, you should start immediately to establish at least one. The amazing thing about multiple sources of income is that once you establish one or two, you attract other bigger and more lucrative sources into your experience. Consider how you will feel when you open your email and there is eighteen thousand unexpected dollars in your account from automated website purchases. My guess is that you'll be pretty happy and excited. It's those feelings of happiness, excitement and gratitude that attract more of the good stuff into your life.

You should enjoy the benefits of multiple sources of income. When you begin to generate revenue without exchanging time, you give yourself that time to spend creating other streams of income. The cycle repeats blissfully over and over until you find yourself one of those lucky people who spend their days doing what they love and enjoying a life of luxury. Millionaires have always used the multiple source of income strategy to build wealth. Decide how much income you would like to earn during a good night's rest. Set the intention and get busy.

"PROFIT IN BUSINESS COMES FROM REPEAT CUSTOMERS, CUSTOMERS THAT BOAST ABOUT YOUR PROJECT OR SERVICE, AND THAT BRING FRIENDS WITH THEM."

~ W. EDWARDS DEMING

CHAPTER 9

Open the Gates

CONGRATULATIONS! You are almost ready to be a millionaire author. You made it to the final chapter where I am going to share my secrets for opening the gates and letting wealth pour into your life. You now know there is virtually no limit to how much you can earn as an author. You now know there is one-and-a-half trillion dollars being spent annually online and that number grows year after year. You now have the information you need to make decisions about how you will write your book and turn it into a million dollar business. What could stop you now?

Paradigms can stop you now. Paradigms are just a bunch of habits and beliefs that you are not even aware of in many cases. They were likely passed on to you as a child by your parents who probably got them from their parents. You might have heard things like, "Money doesn't grow on trees." or "You don't deserve that." when you were a child. I certainly did. You might not even know you have these beliefs that are sabotaging your chances for real success and fulfillment.

I want to teach you a practical exercise I created that's designed to help you identify your paradigms and limiting beliefs and then eliminate them from your life forever. Once you learn this method, you can use it over and over again. If a nagging little voice tells you that you cannot do, be, or have something, you will be equipped to make that negative voice be quiet again.

This exercise requires you to take a piece of paper and draw a line vertically down the middle. Ask yourself questions to uncover your beliefs. Ask yourself: "What do I believe about money?" or "Do I believe I am worthy of success or being a millionaire author? Then you need to tap into your own inner voice and listen to the negative things you hear. "I don't have the proper education." Or "I need money to make money." or "I am a single mom, I can't afford that." or "I'm already running a business, I don't have time." or "I don't know how to run an online business." Whatever that often not-so-quiet voice in your head says to you when you are getting ready to step out and go for a goal.

Then you write those things down on the left column of the page. If you are a positive person, you might find it difficult to write these words on paper but do it anyway, I promise it will be worth it. Those are the things that block you and hold you back. It's time to release them.

Take a moment to read the things you wrote in the left column and then imagine you are enjoying the successful life of a millionaire and reread those statements and think of their opposite. "I am achieving my goals and I am having fun," "There is more than enough.", "I always have plenty of money to do whatever I want to do", "My business is easily generating millions of dollars in profitable revenue and I am serving the greater good with my brilliance."

Then write down the supportive and loving thoughts in the right column. You may not even believe the words you are writing in the right column, but go ahead and write them anyway. These are your new beliefs that will encourage, guide, and support you.

Tear the page down the middle and safely destroy the left side. Be sure to be completely safe when doing this exercise. Get an empty metal garbage bucket, take it outside where you are not near anything flammable and burn that sheet of paper that holds those paradigms. As you watch them burn, focus on seeing yourself as *The Millionaire Author*. Remember you are releasing your old mindset to make room for your new millionaire mindset!

The next technique I use will show you how to get aligned with the feeling of being that #1 New York Times bestselling author with the multi-million dollar business! It's so important that you identify with whatever you want to create and experience. You must be in vibrational alignment with the good that you desire.

How do you know if you are in vibrational alignment? You are in vibrational alignment when you feel like your desires have already manifested. If I asked you, "On a scale of one to ten with your goal to be a #1 New York Times bestselling author, do you believe you are already there? Do you see and feel it?" How would you answer?

My guess is that you would be a little stuck but you would probably rate your vibrational alignment with your goal at around a five. If you are near the top of the scale, good for you! The goal is to be at a ten all day, every day. When you live your life in complete vibrational alignment, your goals will begin to manifest.

I created little vibrational alignment cards that I carry with me. I keep one on the side of my bed. Every day, I measure my emotions to ensure I am in complete and utter vibrational alignment with my goals. My goal is written on the top in the present tense and I track my vibrational alignment with my goals.

Make your own vibrational alignment cards and begin to track where you are on the scale. Write your goal on your card and ask yourself, "Do I really feel like I am there? Where am I on the vibrational scale?" Then write your answer.

The vibrational alignment tool can make a big difference in your life. It is an incredibly powerful tool that will lead you to a greater understanding of yourself and your paradigms.

There are countless activities you can do to open the gates of abundance. You can beat on your chest to awaken the giant or you can meditate inwardly to untether your soul. It doesn't matter where you land between those two; you just have to do what connects you to the feeling of already being a millionaire author.

The feeling will connect you to the source that has the information you seek. Getting emotionally involved in the goal brings it closer to you. Experiencing success now before it manifests is what will cause success to manifest.

Please understand, you must do more than think about your goal of becoming a millionaire author. You must set a deadline to complete your manuscript and get to work. You must be willing learn how to market your book and launch it to the world. You must b on the marketing. Be willing to step outside your comfort zone and be uncomfortable for a while as you adjust to this new way of thinking. You must be willing to do the things that need to be done that will distinguish you from other authors.

If you develop a millionaire mindset, apply the suggestions for launching your book and follow the ideas I shared in this book, you will be on your way. Put your mind to work for you and direct it towards the attainment of your goal and you will get to where you want to go.

"WE ARE ALL APPRENTICES IN A CRAFT WHERE NO ONE EVER BECOMES A MASTER."

~ ERNEST HEMINGWAY

Conclusion

I WROTE THIS BOOK because my desire is for you to be a successful millionaire author. Use the information in this book as a guide to help you make the decisions that will help you achieve the success you desire.

This book is packed full of priceless information I've gathered from my many years as a successful author and decades as a successful entrepreneur. The information in this book will save you years of wasted effort and thousands of dollars if you apply it to your work.

In addition to the incredibly valuable information I've jammed into this little book, I have compiled a webpage where you can access additional resources. There is a downloadable resource list where you will find the contact information of people I use for my projects and recommend to my clients (http://PeggyMcColl.com/the millionaire-author-event-privatepage/).

You are ready to become a millionaire author. Own it, feel it, become the dream! My belief created my facts and your belief will create yours. Decide now that nothing can stop you and start moving forward. The moment you decide to become the successful author from your dreams, you begin to become the successful author of your dreams.

It's just that simple. Once you begin to work towards your goal with purpose and faith, you will be amazed at your wonderful new life. You will attract the circumstances and things you want and life will just seem to fall into place for you. Things that might have led to challenges before you became a millionaire author just won't seem like a big deal anymore, you will just see opportunity everywhere you go. I know because this is the story of my life.

As you know, my family is my number one priority. I raised my son Michel when I was a single mom and he is the most important part of my life. A few years back, just after Michel graduated from high school and started college, he called me and said, "Mom, we need to talk."

Michel lived in a condo close to the college he attended. He was living approximately a thirty minute drive from my house. I told him to come on over. He arrived and lowered his eyes and all but whispered the words, "Mom, Kayla's pregnant." Michel and Kayla were both eighteen years of age at the time.

I was ecstatic! I was not ecstatic because my teenaged son was becoming a father with his teenaged girlfriend, I was ecstatic because I was becoming a grandmother. I was so filled with joy. I immediately felt the love for my unborn grandchild in that moment.

Michel was surprised by my response and said, "Mom you're happy that your teenager is going to have a baby?" He was scared, both he and his girlfriend were in young. All I could say was, "Please relax honey, I will help you. You can both stay in school and I will help you." I said, "This is going to be the most amazing experience that's ever happened!"

Conclusion

Together, with some investment money my son Michel inherited from my Mom, we bought a nice three-bedroom home and Michel, Kayla, and my grandson James are blissfully happy. Michel is now a homeowner. My son finished his college program, and he owns his own business and Kayla is a certified dental assistant. They are wonderful parents and I am blessed to invest lots of time with my grandson. I am extremely happy.

How do you suppose most people would have responded to such a visit from their teenaged son? I can only imagine. For me, I was overwhelmed with gratitude. I was so grateful for everything in my life and my ability to help my son and his young family. I was overwhelmed with joy because I was going to be a grandmother. I was overwhelmed with love for my child who was about to give me a great blessing. It was truly a magical experience.

Is your life experience filled with joy, love, and magic regardless of the circumstances? It can be. Develop the millionaire mindset and abundance will just seem to follow you wherever you go. You will no longer even notice the petty things that used to annoy you and get you off course. (As a side note, if you are feeling "annoyed" or any other emotion that doesn't feel good, you are blocking the flow of good into your life.) All you will experience is the wonderful and miraculous life the Creator intended you to experience.

Start your day with gratitude and hold on to that feeling all day long. You will quickly attract more reasons to be grateful and the cycle will repeat over and over until you can hardly believe the wonderful life that is yours. Set your goal, act with purpose and faith and the life you seek will start seeking you.

Enjoy the journey to becoming a millionaire author. Relish every victory and learn from the occasional defeat. Life wasn't meant to be fun and when you can grow and learn from every challenge, your life will be filled with love, abundance, and success.

I wish you every blessing as you begin your wonderful journey. I am excited for the possibilities for you and everyone in your life. Please take a moment to share your successes with me. My life's purpose is to make a positive contribution to the lives of millions. If this book has helped you work towards your dream, please let me know. You can contact me through my website: http://PeggyMcColl.com.

About the Author

PEGGY MCCOLL, known as The Best Seller Maker, is a New York Times Best Selling Author and an internationally recognized expert in helping authors, entrepreneurs and specialists create valuable products, build their brand worldwide; make money online and create international "best sellers"!

Her intensive classes, speaking engagements, goal achievement seminars, mentoring, and bestselling books have inspired individuals, professional athletes, authors and organizations to reach their maximum potential. Her personal goal is to make a positive contribution to the lives of millions and she is passionate about helping others to achieve their goals.

As a happy wife to Denis, a proud mother of her son Michel and the proudest grandmother of her grandson James, Peggy values her family more than anything! (http://peggymccoll.com)

Made in the USA
Middletown, DE
25 October 2014